A Major Shock

by Paul Stewart
Illustrated by Bill Ledger

OXFORD
UNIVERSITY PRESS

In this story ...

Jin
(Swoop)

Jin has the power to fly. He once had a race with a jumbo jet ... and won! He can even fly high enough to reach outer space!

Ben
(Sprint)

Mr Trainer
(teacher)

The Head
(head teacher)

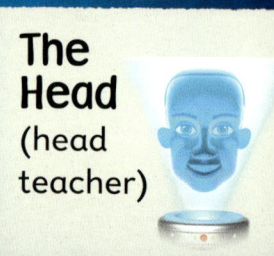

Chapter 1:
Red alert!

"Red alert! Red alert!"

The words boomed out of the speakers all around Hero Academy. The alarm was blaring. Everyone in Mr Trainer's class stopped working.

Ben turned to Jin. "What's happening?" he asked.

"I don't know," replied Jin, "but it sounds serious."

Just then, the alarm fell silent.

The speakers crackled and a deep voice filled the air. It was the Head.

"I've received news of an attack on Lexis City," he announced. "The streets are being flooded with jelly. Someone is trying to bring the city to a standstill. We have to get everyone to safety before the jelly sets."

The heroes all started talking at once.

"A flood of jelly?" questioned Cam.

"That sounds awful ... but delicious!" said Jin.

"I wonder what flavour it is ..." added Ben.

"Get changed, all of you," Mr Trainer said, raising his voice above the din in the classroom.

Within seconds, the children had spun into their superhero costumes.

Jin changed into Swoop and was putting on his mask when Mr Trainer came over.

"Swoop," Mr Trainer said. "The Head wants to see you. Can you go to his office immediately, please?"

Swoop frowned. He wondered what the Head wanted.

As the others set off to deal with the jelly emergency, Swoop went to see the Head. He knocked on the door.

"Enter!" said a voice.

Swoop opened the door and went in.

The Head's glowing hologram face smiled at him warmly. "Swoop," he said, "something very important has come up."

Swoop took a deep breath. He wondered what could be more important than the jelly mission.

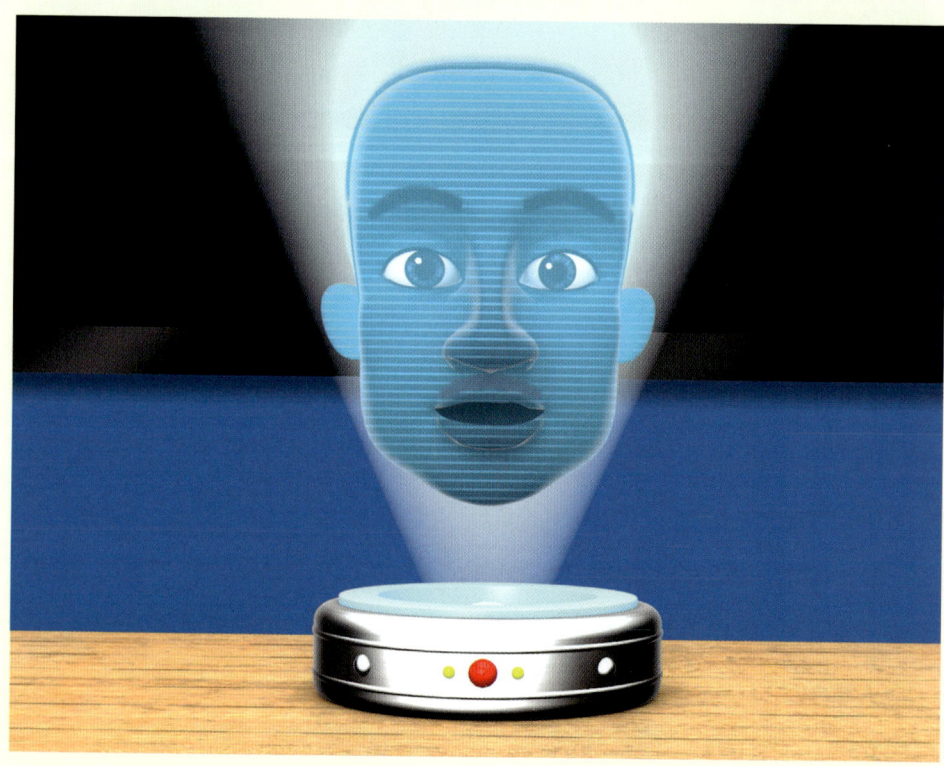

"I've just heard that two inspectors from the Department for Superpowers are coming for a surprise inspection," the Head explained. "I'd like you to show them around."

"Me?" said Swoop.

"You, Swoop," replied the Head. "I'm sure you'd like to go with the others, but this mission is just as important."

"Yes, sir," he said. "I understand."

"Show the inspectors everything they want to see," the Head told Swoop, "but be careful. During the last inspection, Miss Linen demonstrated a silencing gadget that left the inspectors unable to speak for a week." The Head sighed. "We received a warning for that. This time, nothing must go wrong. If they're not happy, they have the power to shut us down. The future of Hero Academy is in your hands."

Swoop gulped.

Chapter 2:
The inspectors

Swoop had just left the Head's office when the front door bell rang.

"That must be the inspectors," Swoop muttered. "I'd better not keep them waiting."

Swoop flew along the corridor as fast as he could.

Swoop opened the front door. A man and woman were standing outside.

The man had red hair and was wearing small, round glasses. He was dressed in a smart jacket and trousers. The woman had dark hair tied up in a bun. She was holding a notebook and pen, and she had a large briefcase with her.

"Good morning," said the man. He looked puzzled. "I thought everyone would be out dealing with the … erm … but never mind."

The man smiled. "We're the school inspectors. I'm Major Scale. This is Lucinda Villiers."

"My name's Swoop," said Swoop politely. "Please come in."

As Swoop led the inspectors through the reception area, he remembered the Head's words. "Nothing must go wrong."

"What would you like to see first?" Swoop asked. "The sports hall? Or maybe the science lab?"

11

"We'd like to see the storerooms," said Lucinda Villiers.

"Oh! OK," Swoop said, trying to hide his surprise.

Major Scale stroked his moustache. "Inspectors can learn a lot from what a school keeps in its storerooms."

"Follow me," said Swoop.

First, he took them to the storeroom in Miss Linen's classroom. It contained boxes of colourful material, buttons, zips and thread used for repairing the superheroes' costumes.

The inspectors weren't impressed.

Swoop took them to Mrs Molten's classroom and showed them her storeroom. On one side of the storeroom, there was a locked glass cabinet full of liquids and powders that Mrs Molten used in her science experiments. On the other side, there were shelves of batteries, switches, plugs and wires.

"Are there any more storerooms?" asked Lucinda Villiers, impatiently.

"There's the sports hall storeroom," said Swoop. "And the kitchen storeroom where—"

"Are there any storerooms which contain gadgets?" Major Scale interrupted.

Swoop frowned. The question seemed a bit odd. Then again, the Head had told him to show the inspectors everything they wanted to see.

"There's a storeroom in Corridor B12," Swoop said. "It contains gadgets that were confiscated from villains."

"Very interesting!" said Major Scale, raising a bushy eyebrow. "Make a note, Miss Villiers."

Confiscated Gadgets Storeroom

The Confiscated Gadgets Storeroom is where the Head puts all the gadgets he has taken from baddies over the years.

Most dangerous gadget: the **Time Wobbler** – used by Mr Minute to time-travel.

Most mysterious gadget: **Gadget Number 261** – taken from Colonel Cortex in Egypt ten years ago. The Head is still trying to discover what it actually does.

Silliest gadget: the **Hover Umbrella** – with its spinning spokes, it can spin you around in the air until you're helpless with laughter.

"Unfortunately, I don't have a key for the Confiscated Gadgets Storeroom," Swoop said. "It's out of bounds for pupils. I could see if there are any teachers around who could let you in?" he added helpfully.

Major Scale shook his head. "Maybe another time." He turned away and whispered something to Lucinda Villiers, who hurried off along the corridor.

Swoop swallowed uneasily.

Chapter 3:
Break in!

"I think I'd like to see that kitchen storeroom after all. Why don't you show it to me, Swoop?" said Major Scale. He patted his stomach. "I'm feeling a bit peckish."

The two of them were halfway to the kitchen when the school alarm went off for a second time that day.

"What now?" Swoop wondered.

"Is there a fire drill?" asked Major Scale, innocently.

Suddenly, the Head's voice blared out of the speakers again. "Someone has broken into the Confiscated Gadgets Storeroom," he announced. "All available staff and pupils must go to Corridor B12."

Swoop gasped. Was that where Lucinda Villiers had gone? Surely an inspector from the Department for Superpowers wouldn't break into the Confiscated Gadgets Storeroom. At least, not a *real* inspector …

"Sorry, I've got to go," Swoop told Major Scale.

"Oh no you don't," said Major Scale.

Dodging the Major's outstretched hands, Swoop took off and flew down the corridor.

"I'll have those gadgets for myself!" Major Scale shouted after him. "And there's nothing that you or anyone else in Hero Academy can do to stop me!"

Swoop flew on, past the empty classrooms, past the sports hall and up a flight of stairs.

The sound of Major Scale's voice grew fainter, then disappeared.

Up on the first floor, Swoop glided round a corner and into Corridor B12.

The Confiscated Gadgets Storeroom had a thick metal door, held shut by a chunky padlock – except now, the door was wide open. Swoop peered inside … and gasped. Apart from cobwebs and thick dust, the shelves were all empty.

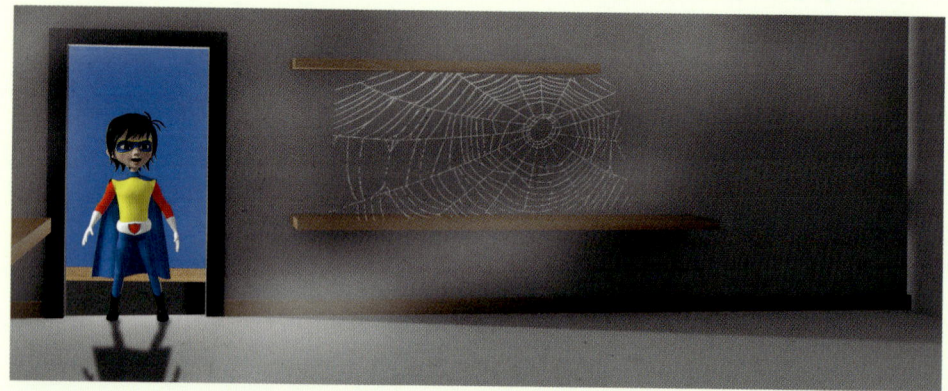

Swoop instantly saw why. Lucinda Villiers was standing on the far side of the room, holding a large bag. It was bulging with all the gadgets she had stolen.

"Give me that bag," said Swoop, trying to sound braver than he felt.

"Come and get it," Lucinda Villiers sneered. She rummaged in the bag. "What shall I use against you? The Mind-control gadget? The Ice-blaster? Or how about this?" she said, taking an object from the bag. "Er … whatever it is."

Swoop knew exactly what the eight-armed gadget in her hands was. It was the Octo-tickler. If he could trick Lucinda Villiers into switching it on, then maybe ...

At that moment, Miss Baker and Mrs Butterworth arrived, out of breath. Miss Baker was brandishing a saucepan and Mrs Butterworth was clutching a frying pan. Mr Trainer followed close behind, with a tennis racket in his hand.

"Get back!" Lucinda Villiers hissed.

"Yes, over by the wall, all of you!" another voice commanded.

It was Major Scale. In his hands was a gadget that Swoop hadn't seen before. It was a yellow box with a rubber nozzle and a big red button.

"What's that?" Swoop asked.

"It's one of *my* gadgets," said Major Scale, with a sly smile. "I call it … the Mega-splatter."

Chapter 4:
The Mega-splatter

Major Scale took aim, pressed the red button and ... *SPLAT!* Swoop was suddenly covered from head to toe in a gloopy, yellow liquid. He wiped it from his face, licked his lips, and his eyebrows shot up with surprise. "Custard!" he said, and snorted. "What a useless gadget!"

Major Scale puffed out his chest and clenched his fists. His face reddened. "Useless gadget? ... USELESS gadget?!"

"It's a first attempt," Lucinda Villiers snapped. "We're just testing it."

"I don't care what you think of my Mega-splatter," Major Scale muttered crossly. "With all these confiscated gadgets, I shall conquer Lexis City!" He turned to Lucinda Villiers. "Take the gadgets and go," he told her. "I'll deal with this lot."

"No!" Swoop cried.

As Lucinda Villiers headed for the door, Major Scale fired the Mega-splatter. Miss Baker caught a big dollop of custard in her saucepan. Mrs Butterworth batted away another dollop with her frying pan. Mr Trainer tried to do the same with his tennis racket but ended up covered in custard.

Soon, the whole floor was awash with custard. It was thick and sticky and very, very slippery.

Miss Baker fell over first, then Mrs Butterworth. When Mr Trainer tried to help them up, he fell over as well.

The only person not having any problems was Swoop … he was up in the air.

Swoop dived down towards Lucinda Villiers who was near the door. He was about to snatch the bag of gadgets from her when – *SPLAT!* – a huge dollop of custard hit him in the chest. He flew backwards through the air and crashed on to the floor.

Lucinda Villiers laughed. "You'll never stop us!"
Swoop groaned. He'd failed …

Then something happened. Something lucky.
As Lucinda Villiers was making her getaway, she
slipped on the puddle of custard and let go of the
bag. It flew up into the air.

Swoop took off like a rocket and caught the
bag in mid-air. Then he zoomed over Major Scale's
head, through the open door and back along
the corridor.

There was an open window at the end of the corridor. Swoop flew through the gap then out over the school sports pitch carrying the bag of gadgets. The two fake inspectors ran outside after him.

"Come back!" Major Scale roared.

"No way," Swoop yelled back.

Just then, there was the sound of sirens.

"The Head called the police," Mr Trainer shouted, from the back door.

Major Scale dropped his Mega-splatter, then turned and fled. "Let's get out of here!" he screamed.

Lucinda Villiers sprinted after him.

"Inspectors, indeed!" said Mr Trainer, as Swoop landed next to him.

"I thought they were acting suspiciously," said Swoop, carefully putting down the bag of confiscated gadgets.

"You did very well, Swoop," said Mr Trainer. "Now, could you return those gadgets to the storeroom, please? Oh, and Swoop," he added, picking up the Mega-splatter. "You'd better take this with you too."

An hour later, the other heroes returned from Lexis City. By then, the Confiscated Gadgets Storeroom had been cleaned, the door repaired, and all the gadgets were safely locked up inside.

"What happened in the city?" Swoop asked Sprint.

Sprint pulled a face. "Nothing. It was a false alarm. It must have been someone playing a trick."

Swoop frowned. "I bet I can guess who that was. So there wasn't any jelly after all?"

Sprint shook his head.

"That's a shame," said Swoop, laughing. "We had some lovely custard to go with it!"